50
UNDERGROUND STATIONS

By Colin Pitt

ISBN 978-1-7398450-6-3

CP PRESS

Published August 2022

Distributed in the U. S. A. by:
SCB Distributors,
15608 South New Century Drive,
Gardena, CA 90248,
U. S. A.

Contents

1. Boston Manor Underground Station, Boston Manor Road, Brentford, Middlesex. TW8 9LQ.

P O' JOE • COFFEE
BOSTON MANOR STATION

2. Park Royal Underground Station, Western Avenue, London. W5 3EL.

UNDERGROUND
UNDERGROUND
24HR MINICABS
PARK ROYAL STATION

3. Alperton Underground Station, Ealing Road, Wembley, Middlesex. HA0 4LL.

ALPERTON STATION
No parking
Offenders will be prosecuted

4. Sudbury Town Underground Station, Station Approach, Wembley, Middlesex. HA0 2LA.

SUDBURY TOWN STATION
UNDERGROUND

5. Sudbury Hill Underground Station, Greenford Road, Harrow, Middlesex. HA1 3RA.

UNDERGROUND
SUDBURY HILL STATION

6. South Harrow Underground Station, South Hill Avenue, Harrow, Middlesex. HA2 8HN.

SOUTH HARROW STATION
Ticket Stop

D
OFF
A

7. Rayner's Lane Underground Station, Rayner's Lane, Harrow, Pinner. HA5 5EG.

Wed in Style
UNDERGROUND
RAYNERS LANE STATION

RAYNERS LANE

Way out ↗
Eastbound platform 2 ↗
PLATFORM
Metropolitan and Piccadilly lines
Westbound platform 1
Rayners Lane
Eastcote
Ruislip Manor
Ruislip
Ickenham
Hillingdon
Uxbridge
tedious
"the dog
Pleo

8. Baron's Court Underground Station, Pallister Road, London. W14 9DA.

BARONS COURT
STATION
RAILWAY
METRO CAFE

TICKETS

EXIT

9. Manor House Underground Station, Greens Lane, London. N4 1BZ.

LIC
UNDERGROUND
SUBWAY
MANOR HOUSE STATION
MANOR HOUSE
DRY CLEANER + LAUNDERERS
MANOR HOUSE STATION

10. Wood Green Undergound Station, High Road, Wood Green, London. N22 4HH.

UNDERGROUND
WOOD GREEN STATION
UNDERGROUND
N J ENTERPRISE
TO TRAINS

11. Bound's Green Underground Station, Bounds Green Road, London. N11 2EV.

UNDERGROUND
telephone
telephone
BREKKY
FASTCASH
cash withdrawals
cash withdrawals
FOOD CENTRE

12. Arnos Grove Underground Station, Bowes Road, London. N11 1AN.

UNDERGROUND
ARNOS GROVE
No
parking
Offenders
will be
prosecuted
SEE IT.
SAY IT.
SORTED.

13. Southgate Underground Station, High Street, London. N14 5BH.

Piccadilly line
← Westbound platform 2
Piccadilly line
Eastbound platform 1 →

14. Cockfosters Underground Station, Cockfosters Road, Barnet. EN4 0DZ.

TICKETS
TICKETS AND INFORMATION
No e-scooters or e-unicycles

TO COCKFOSTERS ROAD
PUBLIC TELEPHONES
TO CAR PARK
COCKFOSTERS CAR SERVICE
CUSHMAN & WAKEFIELD
SHOP
TO LET
020 7935 5000

15. Morden Underground Station, London Road, Morden, Surrey. SM4 5AZ.

Help point

Emergency exit

16. South Wimbledon Underground Station, High Street London. SW19 3DB.

UNDERGROUND
WIMBLEDON

17. Colliers Wood Underground Station, Colliers Wood High Street, London. SW19 2HR.

UNDERGROUND
UNDERGROUND
COLLIERS WOOD STATION
BE KIND
CHRISTCHURCH ROAD, S.W.19

18. Tooting Broadway Underground Station, Tooting High Street, London. SW17 0SU.

TOOTING BROADWAY
UNDERGROUND
TOOTING BROADWAY STATION
free cash withdrawals

19. Tooting Bec Underground Station, Balham High Road, London. SW17 9AH.

UNDERGROUND
Keep left

20. Balham Underground Station, Balham High Road, London. SW12 9BW.

0208 675 4040
BRIDGE ELECTRICIANS
Way out
High Road (west)
Way out
Chestnut Grove

21. Clapham South Underground Station, Balham Hill, London. SW12 9DU.

PEAKY
BLINDERS

22. Clapham Common Underground Station, The Pavement, London. SW4 7AJ.

22. Clapham Common Underground Station, The Pavement, London. SW4 7AJ.

Clapham Common station has a domed roof and a 'To The Trains' sign.

23. Clapham North Underground Station, Clapham High Street, London. SW4 7TS.

BRIXTON

24. Battersea Power Station Underground Station, Battersea Park Road, London. SW8.

1 Edgware
2 High Barnet
Plat 2
07:30:03
Stand on the right
Hold the handrail
Keep clear of the edges
Take extra care with children
Dogs must be carried
No smoking

25. Elephant and Castle Underground Station, London Road, Elephant and Castle, London. SE1 6LW.

G CAFÉ
WE USE LAVAZZA FRESH COFFEE BEANS
0207 407 0107
G NEWS
ELEPHANT & CASTLE STATION

26. Lambeth North Underground Station, 110 Westminster Bridge, London. SE1 7XG.

UNDERGROUND
LAMBETH NORTH STATION
London Borough of Lambeth
WESTMINSTER
BRIDGE ROAD
SE1
SAP

27. Regent's Park Underground Station, Marylebone Road, London. NW1 5HA.

No entry
to lifts from
this side
Southbound platform 2

REGENT'S PARK
·REGENTS·PARK·

28. Edgware Road Underground Station, Chapel Street, London. NW1 5DH.

EDGWARE ROAD STATION
Lycamobile
Call the world for less
TRISHNA NEWS
• OFF LICENCE • DRINKS
• NEWS & MAGS • TOBACCO
• CONFECTIONERY • GREETING CARDS
Bakerloo line
EDGWARE ROAD STATION
Bakerloo line
RVP

29. Paddington Underground Station, Westminster, London. W2 1AE.

29. Paddington Underground Station, Westminster, London. W2 1AE.

PADDINGTON STATION
PADDINGTON STATION
eurochange
bureau de change
Regent
Dry Cleaners
WESTERN UNION
MONEY TRANSFER
UNDERGROUND
PADDINGTON STATION
LFB
RVP
PADDINGTON STATION

30. Warwick Avenue Underground Station, Warwick Avenue, London. W9 2PT.

UNDERGROUND
WARWICK AVENUE STATION
GIVE WAY

31. Maida Vale Underground Station, Elgin Avenue, London. W9 1JS.

UNDERGROUND
STATION
UNDERGROUND
MAIDA VALE STATION
MAIDA VALE
QUALITY COFFEE
FOOD AND CAKE
MAIDA VALE STATION
BananaTree
PAN ASIAN KITCHEN
RANDOLPH AVENUE W9
CITY OF WESTMINSTER
LOOK RIGHT

UNDERGROUND
UNDERGROUND

32. Kilburn Park Underground Station, Cambridge Avenue, London. NW6 5AD.

KILBURN
PARK
EXIT
UNDERGROUND
KILBURN
PARK
ENTRANCE

Bakerloo line

33. Southwark Underground Station, 68-70 Blackfriars Road, London. SE1 8JZ.

SOUTHWARK
STATION
UNDERGROUND
METRO

34. Hanger Lane Underground Station, Hanger Lane, London. W5 1DL.

HANGER LANE STATION

HANGER LANE
0208 998 9910
FLEXIBLE WORKFORCE SOLUTIONS
DRIVERS WANTED

35. Redbridge Underground Station, Eastern Avenue, Ilford, Essex. IG4 5DQ.

UNDERGROUND

36. Loughton Underground Station, Old Station Road, Roding Road, Loughton, Essex. IG10 4PD.

LOUGHTON STATION
Raysam
No parking
Offenders will be prosecuted

37. Temple Underground Station, Victoria Embankment, London. WC2R 2PH.

TEMPLE STATION
Tickets
RVP
METRO

38. Embankment Underground Station, Villiers St., London. WC2N 6NS.

UNDERGROUND
EMBANKMENT
NEVER PAY MORE

39. South Kensington Underground Station, Pelham St., London. SW7 2NB.

SOUTH KENSINGTON

TREATS
Wine & Spirits
Dairy Products
Groceries
TREATS
CARDS GALORE
ANGLO PERSIAN
Planned closures
STOP

UNDERGROUND

GREAT STORIES UNFOLD...
Excite your imagination

Way out
Royal College of Music
Science Museum
Royal Albert Hall
Hyde Park
Imperial College

40. Gloucester Road Underground Station, Gloucester Road, London. SW7 4SF.

GLOUCESTER ROAD STATION
eurochange
Bureau de Change
138
FLOWERS INC
020
7373
3041
FLOWERS INC
OPEN 7 DAYS

41. Chiswick Park Underground Station, Bollo Lane, Chiswick, London. W4 5NE.

PARK STATION
PARK STATION
BORTHWIC
TICKETS
TICKETS

42. Warren Street Underground Station, Tottenham Court Road, London. NW1 3AA.

UNDERGROUND
WARREN STREET STATION
WARREN STREET STATION
LFB
WIZZ AWAY
"A BRILLIANT
SHOW CELEBRATING
MARLEY'S
GENIUS"
UP!
THE BOB
MARLEY
MUSICAL

43. Mornington Crescent Underground Station, Eversholt St., London. NW1 2JA.

MORNINGTON CRESCENT STATION
UNDERGROUND
MORNINGTON CARS
Licensed by the P.C.O.
DRIVERS WANTED

44. Chalk Farm Underground Station, Adelaide Rd., Chalk Farm, London. NW3 2BP.

UNDERGROUND
CHALK FARM STATION
UNDERGROUND
LFB

45. Hampstead Underground Station, Hampstead High Street, London. NW3 1QG.

COFFEEhead
FRESH GROUND COFFEE
Please use shop inside the station
ICED COFFEE
HAMPSTEAD STATION
RVP
Trains from Hampstead

46. Kentish Town Underground Station, Kentish Town Road, London. NW5 2AA.

KENTISH TOWN
KENTISH TOWN STATION
KENTISH TOWN
STAT ON
BUS STOP

47. Highgate Underground Station, Archway Rd., London. N6 5UA.

HIGHGATE STATION

48. East Finchley Underground Station, High Road, London. N2 0NW.

EAST F

49. Victoria Underground Station, Victoria Street, London. SW1E 5ND.

UNDERGROUND
Lift
Victoria
Underground
Station

50. Great Portland Street Station, Great Portland Street, London. W1W 5PP.

GREAT PORTLAND STREET STATION
GREAT PORTLAND STREET
GOLDEN NEWS
WE SELL TOBACCO HERE

TRAINS